LiftLog

Diary and Guide for Strength Training

Third Edition

Tim Houts

McGraw·Hill

New York   Chicago   San Francisco   Lisbon   London   Madrid   Mexico City
Milan   New Delhi   San Juan   Seoul   Singapore   Sydney   Toronto

Library of Congress Cataloging-in-Publication Data

Houts, Tim.
    Liftlog : diary & guide for strength training / Tim Houts. —3rd ed.
       p.   cm.
    Rev. ed. of: Liftlog / Nate Foster, Tim Houts. 2nd ed.
    Includes bibliographical references.
    ISBN 0-07-145936-7 (alk. paper)
    1. Weight training.   I. Title: Lift log.   II. Foster, Nate. Liftlog.   III. Title.

   GV546.F67   2006
   613.7'13—dc22   2005010068

3 4 5 6 7 8 9 0 DOC/DOC 0 9 8 7

ISBN 0-07-145936-7

Interior design by Think Design Group, LLC
Interior photographs by Ian Spanier

McGraw-Hill books are available at special quantity discounts to use as premiums and sales promotions, or for use in corporate training programs. For more information, please write to the Director of Special Sales, Professional Publishing, McGraw-Hill, Two Penn Plaza, New York, NY 10121-2298. Or contact your local bookstore.

This book is printed on acid-free paper.

Contents

Introduction v

Training Guide 1

  Warm-Up and Stretching 3

  Nutrition 101 5

  Defining and Setting Goals 8

  Strength Training Basics 10

  Major Muscle Groups 13

  Conditioning 101 15

  Organizing Your Workouts 17

  Sample Workouts 21

  Getting the Most Out of Your Diary 29

Training Diary 35

Additional Resources 165

Introduction

Welcome to *LiftLog*, a tool to help you turn your fitness and strength training goals into reality!

By using this log, you've already taken the first step on your training journey. Somebody once said, "If you don't know where you're going, how can you expect to get there?" Kind of funny, but true!

LiftLog will help you map your training destination and track your progress along the way, so if you get detoured, you can get back on track. Not only will you know where you want to go, but you'll know if the path you've taken is moving you in the right direction, and you'll know when you get there.

I hope you enjoy *LiftLog*'s features:

> **Training guide.** This 34-page guide provides some training basics like workout organization, goal setting, and progression, as well as several sample workouts that can provide starting points for every level, from beginner to advanced.

> **Easy-to-use diary pages.** In this edition, I've taken time to make the easy-to-use diary pages even better. The pages still give you plenty of room to note your sets, reps, and weights for each workout, as well as cardio and conditioning. In addition, there is now a section where you can make notes on your nutritional program, and summary pages have been added to review your progress every 14 days. And, finally, the page design has been freshened up to add a little more visual interest. I hope these pages take you where you want to go!

> **Motivational photos.** As in previous editions, there are a host of remarkable photos throughout the book that I hope will

inspire and motivate you and help you keep your training on track all the way to your fitness goal.

> **Additional resources.** To help you progress even more, the Additional Resources section lists books, periodicals, and Internet resources that offer more in-depth information on strength training, nutrition, and fitness, as well as Internet services that can help you locate a personal trainer.

Train well. Eat well. Live great.

Training Guide

Warm-Up and Stretching

You've probably heard it a thousand times before: warm up and stretch before each workout and cool down and stretch after. Well, count this as a thousand and one.

Warming up and stretching at the beginning of your workout helps prevent injury and improve performance by increasing muscle and joint flexibility and blood flow. An end-of-workout cooldown and stretch helps your body redistribute blood and carry out lactic acid, which reduces muscle soreness and tightening and helps you get ready for your next workout.

Warm-Up and Cooldown

Both the warm-up and cooldown are key to keeping your body injury-free and high performing. Build 10 to 15 minutes into the beginning of your workout schedule for the warm-up and 10 to 15 minutes at the end to cool down. Use activities that are continuous and that progress gradually to a low to moderate intensity for warm-up and cooldown, including treadmill, elliptical machine, stationary bike, or even running.

Stretching

Stretching as part of your warm-up and cooldown will improve your range of movement and enhance your body's overall performance. To get the most from your stretching, choose stretches that focus on the major joints and connective tissue areas such as shoulders, back, hips, knees, and ankles. When you do your stretching movements, concentrate on moving slowly, gradually, and smoothly. Never force, bounce, or strain to reach stretch positions. Hold each stretch for 15 to 30 seconds, then repeat. There are many stretching styles and movements, but the basics work best.

> **Chest pull.** Stand facing a door frame. Place your hands on the frame at shoulder level and walk through the doorway until you feel tension in your chest muscles. Or, have your training partner stand behind you and gently pull your arms behind your back in the same motion.
> **Side bends.** Stand with your feet shoulder-width apart. Extend one arm overhead and place the hand of your other arm on your hip. Bend toward the opposite side from your lifted arm, then repeat on both sides.
> **Thigh stretch.** Lie on your left side with your head resting on your left hand. With your right hand, hold your right foot between your toes and ankle joint and pull your heel toward your buttocks. Repeat on the opposite side.
> **Alternate quad stretch.** Stand facing a wall. Hold one foot between your toes and ankle joint as you bend your leg and gently pull the bottom of your foot toward your buttocks. Repeat on each side.
> **Hamstring stretch.** Sit on the floor with your legs straight out in front of you, knees flat, toes pointed up, hands on your thighs. Now bend slowly from the waist toward your toes and exhale. Repeat this movement several times.
> **Back stretch.** Lie flat on your back on the floor with your legs extended. Use your hands to pull your right knee up to your chest. Repeat with your left knee, then with both knees.

Add to or adjust the focus of your stretching exercises to match the muscle groups you're working in your strength training program. Remember, make stretching a habit, and you'll have a more flexible body that is less prone to injury, runs more smoothly, and recovers faster.

Nutrition 101

Good, sound nutrition is a critical element to any training program. And it only makes sense, doesn't it? Nutrition— your diet, what you eat morning, noon, and night—is your body's fuel. It's what your body uses to build muscle (and more) from your workouts. Great training plus great diet equals great body. Yet, because you don't do your eating in the gym, it's easy to forget about nutrition as part of your training. Don't. Nutrition is 60 percent of your strength training success.

While it seems new nutritional trends and theories are published every other week, remember to take these latest and greatest findings with a grain of salt. One week carbohydrates or protein are in, and the next they're out. Consider using the basic nutritional guidelines as a cornerstone for your diet, while allowing yourself to try alternatives in moderation and, ultimately, finding what works best for you.

Fuel yourself well with a balanced diet, with a keen eye on four key areas: carbohydrates, proteins, fats, and vitamins and minerals.

Carbohydrates

Complex carbohydrates provide an excellent source of highly burnable "fuel" for strength training and can be a good source of protein, vitamins, and minerals. Normal dietary guidelines suggest you make carbohydrates 50 to 60 percent of your daily caloric intake. While strength training, you may consider lowering this percentage slightly and increasing your protein intake to make up the difference to meet your body's need for extra protein to build muscle tissue.

Carbohydrates include potatoes, whole grain rice and pasta, kasha, corn, peas, beans, and fruits and vegetables.

Proteins

Proteins are essential to build muscle tissue, ligaments, tendons, and bones. While normal dietary guidelines suggest you make proteins 15 percent of your caloric intake, consider making proteins a higher percentage while strength training. Here's a quick formula for calculating daily protein needs: consume 1 gram of protein for every 2.2 pounds of body weight. For example, a 150-pound person would need 68 grams of protein (150 ÷ 2.2 = 68.1). But remember that any excess protein will be converted into fat.

Choose lean sources of proteins such as turkey, skinless chicken, fish, and egg whites. Other proteins include meats, poultry, fish, cheese, beans and legumes, and whole grains.

Fats

Fats, in limited quantity, are important to your body makeup. However, many foods contain hidden fats, so be aware of all the fats you consume. Fats, ounce for ounce, contain twice the calories of proteins or carbohydrates. Limit your fat intake to 25 to 30 percent of your caloric intake.

Most packaged food labels today note the percentage of calories from fat. If the label doesn't show the percentage of fat calories, look for the fat content in grams. Since there are 9 calories per gram of fat, search for foods that have fewer than three grams of fat per 100 total calories (3 fat grams × 9 calories each = 27 fat calories, which would equal 27 percent fat calories in 100 total calories).

Watch your total fat intake, and for heart-healthy fats, avoid foods that are high in saturated and trans fats, such as butter, cheese, whole milk products, and fried foods. Look to replace these fats with those that are high in unsaturated fats and low in cholesterol, such as olive oil, natural peanut butter, and avocadoes.

Vitamins and Minerals

Eating a well-balanced diet with plenty of fruits and vegetables can provide all the vitamins and minerals your body needs to stay strong and healthy. Take a look at these examples of tasty sources of vitamins and minerals:

> **Vitamin C**, key for rebuilding tissue and preventing illness, is found in abundance in grapefruits, oranges, mangos, papayas, strawberries, blackberries, raspberries, tomatoes, green peppers, broccoli, and cauliflower.
> **Calcium**, critical for building strong bones and bodies, is easily found in milk, yogurt, cheese, soy milk, collard greens, broccoli, figs, and beans.
> **Iron**, important to prevent anemia, is plentiful in duck, beef, oysters, pumpkin, potatoes (with skin), spinach, legumes, and soybeans and soy products.

Even with most nutrient needs available in a balanced diet, you may choose to consider supplements to offset any deficiencies in your diet. But move cautiously. Your body is designed by nature to work with what's available in nature as whole foods. Study up before you jump into the latest vitamin or supplement program. Try programs in moderation, note how you feel in your training log, and evaluate your program to be sure it's getting you what you're after. What works and is safe for others may not be for you.

Review Your Diet

To see if your diet is balanced and full of all the nutrients you need, track your diet for one week every six to nine months. See if you're getting 55 to 60 percent of your calories from carbohydrates, 15 percent from proteins, and 25 to 30 percent from fats. Then, adjust your diet accordingly based on what you find. Consider tracking your diet more frequently if you find it far off your goals.

Defining and Setting Goals

I t's easy to set out on a workout program without a clear destination. And without a clear destination, it is, by definition, impossible to get there.

You might say, "Hey, I've got a destination. I've got a goal. I want to get in shape!" Do you mean in shape for a middle-aged executive, or in shape for a pro athlete? Obviously, they're wholly different.

Take the time to spell out your goals in detail. The more specific you can be in defining your goals, the easier it will be to map how to get there and the more satisfying when you reach them.

Setting Goals

In setting your goals, think of fitness as a state of well-being consisting of optimum levels of strength, flexibility, weight control, and cardiovascular and aerobic capacities that help you participate fully in life. Customize the levels you set for your fitness goals to *your* overall life and fitness goals.

To make your goals the most helpful, make them focused, realistic, and measurable.

Focused

Take a moment to think about why you're training and what it means to you. Are you training to address specific health or injury issues? Are you training to support another sports activity? Are you trying to get in shape for work or career reasons? Whatever your reasons, understand them and use them to tailor your training to meet your ultimate goal focus.

Realistic

Set your goals so they are realistic and reachable. The idea of goal-setting is to give you wins and successes that will motivate you to reach larger goals.

Maximize your training time by noting goals in your diary and reviewing them each day before you train. Break your ultimate goals into subgoals and tactics. Set short-term goals you can reach in 30 days, then set midterm goals to reach in 90 days, and finally set long-term goals that run from six to 12 months. Remember that the more time you put into your planning, the more you'll get out of your training.

Measurable

Whatever your goal, if it isn't measurable you won't know when you're there. "Getting in shape" isn't measurable. "A 32-inch waist, 165 pound body weight, five workouts per week" is. Before starting your strength training, measure your body top to bottom. Record the information in the Body Measurement Worksheet (located just before the beginning of the daily workout log). Update that page regularly to see your progress. Note other goals and check them regularly. It'll get you to your destination, and it's gonna feel great when you get there!

Strength Training Basics

The human body begins to lose muscle tissue at a rate of a half to one pound per year after the age of thirty. Muscle tissue becomes both smaller and weaker as we age. That is, unless we do something about it.

Find a strength training program to do at least two to three times per week to help you decrease body fat, increase muscle tissue, develop strength, maintain strong bones, and keep up a better overall appearance. Incorporate the following basic weight-training principles in your program.

Strength Overload

When muscles are continually forced to lift, push, or pull a weight, they will respond by building size and strength to handle the demands. Set your workouts to overload each muscle group by doing enough sets and repetitions of each exercise to reach the point of muscle failure. Muscle failure is the point where the muscles cannot complete another lift, pull, or push.

Sets and Repetitions

Sets are groupings of a series of repeated exercises or *repetitions* (reps). Organize your workouts into sets and repetitions to get the most from your efforts. Adjust your sets and repetitions according to how heavy a weight is being lifted. Do fewer repetitions of heavier weights and more repetitions of lighter weights. Adjust the number of sets based on your level of fitness and the number of repetitions per set. Do sets and repetitions from one set of 15 repetitions to five sets of 8 to 12 repetitions.

How Much Weight to Use

Experiment with different weight levels to choose the right weight. Pick a weight poundage that allows you to complete all the sets and repetitions asked for in your program. The weights should not be too heavy or too light. The weights are too heavy if you cannot complete the workout, and they're too light if you breeze through too easily. Sets with lighter weights and more reps can focus your workout on building muscle definition and endurance. Conversely, sets with higher weights and fewer reps can focus your efforts on building muscle mass and strength. Record your progress and review your *LiftLog* to help make adjustments to your goals.

Form Is Key

Remember the importance of form in your strength training programs. Form can be the difference between positive results and no results. Proper form will also help prevent strength training injuries and help develop balance, coordination, and flexibility. Ask your club's personal trainer for tips on your form.

Progression

Strive for progression with each strength training session weekly. That is, try to increase either the repetitions or the resistance (weights) in one or more exercise each session. If your program calls for 8 to 12 repetitions, for example, then anytime you can do more than 12 reps, increase your weight by about 5 percent. Beginners should strive to make a 5 percent increase in all exercises each week. Intermediate to advanced trainees should focus on a 5 percent increase in each exercise every two weeks or 10 percent per month. Remember that percentage increases will vary from exercise to exercise, body part to body part, and from individual to individual. Customize your progression to your body and your program, but remember that progression is the key to improvement.

FIT

To get the greatest benefits from your strength training exercises and workouts, concentrate on three key factors: frequency, intensity, and time.

> **Frequency** is how often you train per week. Remember that you cannot store fitness. Strength train at least two or three days per week and up to five days if possible.

> **Intensity** is how hard you exert yourself during the training sessions. Find an intensity level that increases your heart rate and breathing. Adjust your level of intensity to how you feel each training day. Remember to work hard, but not beyond your ability, training, or recovery level. Set your intensity pace by the clock based on 30- to 60-second rest intervals between sets for the upper body and 60 to 120 seconds for the lower body. Find the level of training intensity best for you. Begin with moderate intensity and increase as you improve.

> **Time** is how long your training sessions take. As a beginner, spend about 30 minutes strength training and gradually increase the time over 30 days. Work toward a minimum of 45 minutes and build toward 60- to 90-minute workouts with short rest intervals.

Major
Muscle Groups

Study the major muscle groups of the human body shown on the next page to help you visualize how each strength training exercise works your muscles. Understand which muscles are used in each exercise and their function. Select and focus your lifting exercises to isolate particular muscle groups.

Incorporate strength training that involves both anterior (front) and posterior (back) muscles to build a balanced body, prevent injury, and build better muscular form and symmetry. Use the following table and illustration to identify major muscle groups and key weight training exercises to use in your workouts.

MUSCLE	*BEST EXERCISES*
1. Trapezius (traps)	Shrugs, upright rows, cleans, lateral raises
2. Deltoids (delts)	Seated press, lateral raises, military press, dumbbell press
3. Pectorals (pecs)	Bench press, incline press, dumbbell press, push-ups, pullovers
4. Latissimus dorsi (lats)	Pulldowns, seated rows, dumbbell rows, pull-ups, barbell rows
5. Biceps	Barbell curls, dumbbell curls, cable curls, chin-ups
6. Abdominals (abs)	Sit-ups, knee-ups, leg raises, twists, crunches
7. Forearms	Wrist curls, reverse curls, gripping objects isometrically
8. Gluteals (buttocks)	Squats, lunges, good mornings

9. Quadriceps (quads)   Squats, leg presses, leg extensions, lunges
10. Hamstrings (hams)   Lunges, leg curls, running stairs, hills, sprinting
11. Gastrocnemius (calves)   Calf raises, calf extensions, seated calf raises

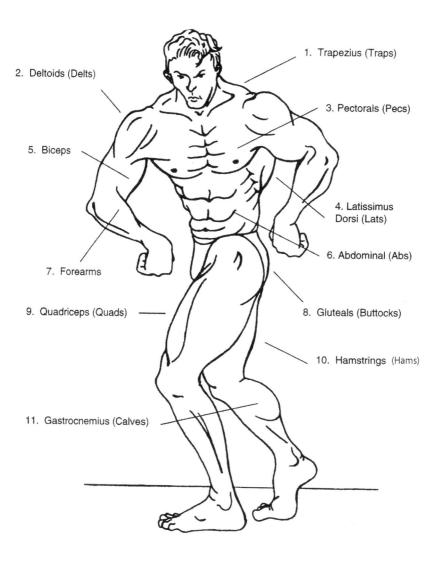

Conditioning 101

Whether you call it conditioning, cardio, or cardio conditioning, it's an important element to your strength training program. Cardio will help your strength training progress more easily and with less chance of injury. A well-conditioned body will work and perform better because of increased ability to carry blood and oxygen to muscles. And remember that cardio burns fat and increases your metabolism to help you stay lean as you build muscle mass.

Choose Cardio That You Like

Choose the cardio exercises that you enjoy. Include at least 20 minutes of conditioning per day, three to five days per week. Good cardio conditioning exercises include walking, jogging, running, cycling, and swimming, or using the treadmill, stationary cycle, stair-climber, elliptical machine, or rowing machine.

Stretch First

Stretch and warm up before and after your conditioning efforts. Use the stretching exercises in this guide to help prevent injury and improve performance. When possible, use cardio training before your strength training workouts as a good warm-up for your lifting workout.

Mix It Up

Mix different cardio conditioning into your training to keep your workouts fresh and help you stay mentally and physically sharp and interested. If you use stationary cycling as your conditioning, for example, get on a mobile bike and enjoy the outdoor scenery once in a while. If you run on the treadmill, take a break and find a different course in the hills, up stairs, along a beach, or through parks to freshen up your program. Grab a pair of cross-country skis or roller or in-line skates and see some sights as you get in shape!

Find ways to enjoy your cardio conditioning as much as your strength training and include it consistently. You'll get a body that will respond better, perform better, and look better.

Organizing Your Workouts

Organize your workouts based on your fitness and strength training goals and the time you have available to train. Group your workouts into either one comprehensive workout that covers the whole body (in less detail) or a series of in-depth workouts that cover parts of the body in greater detail.

If you're just getting started and have less time for your training, you may prefer to organize your training into one comprehensive workout that you would repeat several times per week. If you have more advanced goals and more training time, you may find better results by breaking your workouts according to body part.

Organize by Body Part

The exercises listed below are organized by body part. To create one comprehensive workout that covers the entire body, choose one to two exercises for each body part. To create an in-depth workout, choose three to five exercises for two or three body parts, then focus on different body parts on alternating workout days.

Do sets and repetitions from one set of 15 reps to five sets of 8 to 12 reps.

SHOULDERS

Seated press with barbells or dumbbells

Press behind the neck with barbells

Lateral raise with dumbbells

Upright rows with barbells

Bent-over raises with dumbbells

CHEST

Bench press with barbells or dumbbells

Incline press with barbells or dumbbells

Bent-arm flies with dumbbells

Decline press with dumbbells

Bent-arm pullovers with dumbbells

BACK

Lat pulldown (front, rear)

Seated rows

Bent-over rows with barbells

Reverse dumbbell flies

Pull-ups, wide or narrow grip

Alternate dumbbell rows

ARMS

Barbell curls

Alternate dumbbell curls

Cable curls

Triceps press down on cables

Triceps French press with dumbbells

Triceps kickbacks with dumbbells

ABDOMINAL

Bent-knee crunches

Hanging knee-ups from bar

Leg lifts lying on floor

Side bends with dumbbells

Alternate bent-knee crunches

UPPER LEGS

Squats, barbell or dumbbell

Lunges

Leg extensions

Leg press

Hack squats or press

LOWER LEGS

Standing calf raises

Seated calf raises

Calf raises with leg press

Jumping rope

Stair-climber on your toes for the final three minutes of stepping

Alternate Training Sessions

Choose exercises that work opposing muscle groups and focus on major muscles that may be weaker than others. Alternate your training sessions so that you work the upper body hard and the lower body easy, then the lower body hard and upper body easy. Try training your major muscles in groups.

Comprehensive Workout

As an example of a comprehensive workout, choose exercises that involve all major muscle groups starting from top (shoulders) to bottom (calves). Beginners do one set of 10 to 12 reps from each group, intermediates do three sets of 8 to 10 reps, and advanced lifters complete three to five sets of 8, 10, and 12 reps or 6, 8, and 10 reps. Train your muscle groups using a variety of exercises so that they are subjected to different stimuli. Change your strength training routines every three to four months to maximize results.

In-Depth Workout

As an example of an in-depth workout, do exercises for chest, back, and biceps in one session, then shoulders, abdominals, and legs in the next session.

Sample Workouts

The following are examples of strength training programs for beginning, intermediate, and advanced workouts. The strength training programs include weekly sessions that progress over 12 weeks. Adjust them to fit your needs, goals, schedule, and fitness level. Remember to complete all sets and reps in any given program. Concentrate on range of motion and good form first, and worry about how heavy a weight you're lifting second.

Program 1: Beginning

This is a beginning program for use as a first-time strength training program or as a program to rebuild after a layoff. Ask your club's personal trainer to give you tips on form and weight selection for each exercise.

Weeks 1 to 4

Determine your maximum weight for each exercise. Use 20 to 30 percent of this weight as your training weight. Do each exercise 8 to 10 reps for one set. Do the entire program three times per week, with a day off between efforts.

Increase the number of sets to two for each exercise after the second week. Increase to three sets after the third week.

Weeks 5 to 11

Progress to the following program for weeks 5 to 11. Always adjust your program to your fitness level. Ask your club's personal trainer to give you tips on form and weight selection for each exercise.

Determine your maximum weight for each exercise. Use 40 percent of this weight as your training weight. Do each exercise 12 to 15 reps per set. To make your workout more complete and intense, perform 30 to 45 seconds of aerobic activity such as jogging, stationary cycling, or jump rope between exercises. Do the entire program three times per week, with a day off between efforts.

Increase the number of sets to two for each exercise after the second week. Increase to three sets after the third week. Maintain at three sets.

Exercise	Sets	Reps
Leg press	1–3	12–15
Bench press	1–3	12–15
Leg curls	1–3	12–15
Pulldowns	1–3	12–15
Shoulder press	1–3	12–15
Sit-ups	1–3	Maximum per set
Heel raises	1–3	Maximum per set
Curls	1–3	12–15
Triceps press	1–3	12–15

Program 2: Intermediate

Use this intermediate program if you have some weight-lifting experience or are progressing in your training. Ask your club's personal trainer to help you with your form and weight selection for each exercise.

Weeks 1 to 2

Choose one exercise per body part and do one set of 15 each for the first two weeks.

Weeks 3 to 5

Increase to two exercises per body part for weeks 3 through 5, and increase the number of sets per exercise to two, one set of 15 reps and one of 12. Increase the weight on the second, shorter set. Remember to adjust your program to your fitness level as it changes through your training cycle, and be sure to complete all sets and reps for each exercise.

Weeks 6 to 12

Select three exercises per body part during weeks 6 through 12. Do all sets as listed. Be aware of exercises that become easy and increase your weights as needed, but always complete all sets and reps before increasing weights.

Exercise	Sets	Reps
Back		
Wide-grip pulldowns	3	15-12-10
Seated rows	3	15-12-10
T-bar rows	3	15-12-10
Stiff-legged dead lifts	3	15-12-10
Chest		
Bench press	3	15-12-10
Incline dumbbell press	3	15-12-10
Cable crossovers	3	15-12-10
Dips	3	Maximum
Shoulders		
Military press	3	15-12-10
Lateral raises	3	15-12-10
Bent-over laterals	3	15-12-10
Legs		
Leg extensions	4	16-14-12-10
Squats	4	16-14-12-10
Hack squats	4	16-14-12-10
Leg curls	4	16-14-12-10
Biceps		
Barbell curls	3	15-12-10
Preacher curls	3	15-12-10
Cable concentration curls	2	12-10

Exercise	Sets	Reps
Triceps		
Triceps press downs	4	16-14-12-10
Close-grip bench press	3	15-12-10
Lying triceps extensions	3	15-12-10
One-arm cable press downs	3	15-12-10
Calves		
Standing calf raises	2	20-15
Seated calf raises	2	20-15
Abdominals		
Crunches	2	20-20
Rope crunches	2	20-20
Seated leg tucks	2	20-20

Program 3: Advanced

Use the following schedule and exercises as an advanced work-out. To prevent injury, use this program only after you've built your strength and fitness levels beyond the beginning and intermediate stages. Select your weight levels so you can complete all sets and reps, and adjust the program to your specific strength training and fitness point. Weight levels should be 40 to 60 percent of your maximum. Use this program as a model to develop your own programs as you move through your training cycles.

Exercise	Sets	Reps
Monday		
Abdominals		
Crunches	3–4	25–50
Leg raises	3–4	25–50
Rotary torso	3–4	25–50
Chest		
Bench press	3–4	10–12
Dumbbell incline press	3–4	10–12
One-arm cable crossover	3–4	10–12
Dumbbell pullover	3–4	10–15

Exercise	Sets	Reps
Back		
Wide-grip pulldown	3–4	10–12
Seated lat row	3–4	10–12
Row machine	3–4	10–12
One-arm dumbbell row	3–4	8–10

Conditioning

20 minutes cycling

Tuesday

Abdominal

Repeat Monday

Exercise	Sets	Reps
Shoulders		
Press behind neck	3–4	10-12-8-6
Steep shoulder press	3–4	8–10
Side arm lateral raises	3–4	8–10
Hammer raises	3–4	8–10
Biceps		
Bent bar curls	3–4	8–10
Biceps machine	3–4	8–10
Scott curls	3–4	8–10
Triceps		
Lying triceps extensions	3–4	8–10
Triceps press machine	3–4	8–10
Pulley pushdown	3–4	8–10

Conditioning

20 minutes treadmill

Wednesday

Abdominals

Repeat Monday

Exercise	Sets	Reps
Legs		
Leg extensions	3–4	12–15
Leg curls	3–4	10–12
Leg press/squats	3–4	10–12
Toe raises	3–4	Maximum

Exercise	Sets	Reps
Seated calf raises	3–4	Maximum
Stiff-arm pullovers	3–4	10–12

Conditioning

20 minutes cycling

Thursday

Repeat Monday

Friday

Repeat Tuesday

Saturday

Repeat Wednesday

Sunday

Day off

Program 4: Alternate Advanced Workout

Use the following schedule and exercises as an advanced workout that provides even more focus by body part. To prevent injury, use this program only after you've built your strength and fitness levels beyond the beginning and intermediate stages. Select your weight levels so you can complete all sets and reps, and adjust the program to your specific strength training and fitness point. Weight levels should be 40 to 60 percent of your maximum. Use this program as a model to develop your own programs as you move through your training cycles.

Exercise	Sets	Reps
Monday		
Chest		
Bench press	2	15–15 (warm-up, light weight)
Bench press	3	8–10
Dumbbell incline press	3	8–10
Decline bench press	3	8–10
Cable crossovers	3	8–10

Exercise	Sets	Reps
Calves		
Leg press calf extensions	2	15–15 (warm-up, light weight)
Leg press calf extensions	3	8–10
Seated calf machine (toes out)	3	8–10
Seated calf machine (toes in)	3	8–10

Tuesday

Exercise	Sets	Reps
Shoulders		
Seated dumbbell press	2	15–15 (warm-up, light weight)
Seated dumbbell press	3	8–10
Wide-grip upright rows	3	8–10
Seated side lateral	3	8–10
Bent-over rear laterals	3	8–10
Barbell shrugs	3	8–10
Abdominal		
Machine crunches	3	15–20
Biceps		
Bent bar curls	3–4	8–10
Biceps machine	3–4	8–10
Scott curls	3–4	8–10

Wednesday

Exercise	Sets	Reps
Back		
Wide-grip pulldown to chest	2	15–15 (warm-up, light weight)
Wide-grip pulldown to chest	3	8–10
Close-grip pulldown to chest	3	8–10
Seated rows, wide or close grip	3	8–10
Dumbbell rows	3	8–10
Calves		
Same as Monday		

Thursday

Exercise	Sets	Reps
Triceps		
Close-grip bench press	2	15–15 (warm-up, light weight)
Close-grip bench press	3	8–10
Seated overhead dumbbell press	3	8–10

Exercise	Sets	Reps
Pushdowns	3	8–10
Kickbacks	3	8–10

Biceps

Exercise	Sets	Reps
Standing barbell curls	2	15–15 (warm-up, light weight)
Standing barbell curls	3	8–10
Seated dumbbell curls	3	8–10
EZ bar preacher bench	3	8–10
Concentration curls	3	8–10

Forearms

Exercise	Sets	Reps
EZ bar reverse grip	3	8–10
Wrist curl palms down	3	8–10

Friday

Legs

Exercise	Sets	Reps
Squats	3	20 (warm-up, light weight)
Squats	3	10–15
Leg press	3	10–15
Leg extensions	3	10–15
Leg curls	3	10–15
Straight-leg dead lift	3	10–15

Abdominal

Same as Tuesday

Saturday

Day off

Sunday

Day off

Getting the Most Out of Your Diary

LiftLog is a tool that can help you get the most out of your training. As with any tool, you can get more out of it when you adjust it to fit yourself and your needs. We've provided plenty of space and flexibility in the diary pages to let you decide what and how much information to record. Whatever you record, making daily notes can be one of the best ways to keep you on track to meeting your goals. Here are a couple of ways to get the most out of your diary.

Adjust to Your Needs

Adjust your notes according to your needs and training focus as you progress through your training cycles. *LiftLog*'s diary page lets you write inside the lines and out. Use the sections to note key training data, but, of course, be sure to make notes on *any* areas that are important to you. For example, you may focus on your diet and body weight during early stages of a training cycle, while later you may focus on sets, reps, and weights (see the sample diary on page 30). Use the page in whatever way works best for you.

Be Consistent

Your diary, like your training, is only as good as what you put into it. Be consistent in recording your training. Remember to record your body weight and measurements every 30 days. And don't forget to note how you feel during and after workouts. This subjec-

DAY 1

- [X] **MONDAY**
- [ ] **TUESDAY**
- [ ] **WEDNESDAY**
- [ ] **THURSDAY**
- [ ] **FRIDAY**
- [ ] **SATURDAY**
- [ ] **SUNDAY**

7/18/05
Date

Warm Up   Treadmill 14 minutes at Level 6

Body Focus/Exercise	SETS	REPS	WEIGHTS
UPPER BODY PROGRAM:			
Abs: bent-knee crunches	4	25	
Back: pull-ups	4	10	
Arms: bar dips	4	10	
Chest: push-ups	4	15	
Shoulders: DB lateral raises	3	10	15
Shoulders: barbell seated press	3	10	85/95/85
Shoulders: upright rows	3	12/10/8	65/75/85
Chest: DB incline flys	3	10	25/30/25
Chest: bench press	3	12/10/8	135/175/185
Chest: DB decline press	3	12/10/8	45/55/65
Back: pulldowns (lats)	3	10	120/130/140
Back: seated rows	3	10	100/110/120
Back: DB alt. rows	3	10/8/6	45/55/65
Arms: barbell curls	3	max reps	75
Arms: DB alt. curls	3	max reps	30/35
Arms: triceps pushdowns	3	max reps	70

Conditioning/Cardio   Cooldown: Lifecycle 12 min. at random 5

Nutrition/Notes   Feeling stronger! Keep up stretching program! Try to increase calories each day next week.

Feeling

tive data can be as valuable as the objective data of sets, reps, and weights.

Review Your Progress

Every two weeks, use the 14-Day Review page to recognize your goals met, summarize your workouts, record your body weight, note any feelings or comments, and set goals for the next 14 days. Look at the exercises completed to determine if your workouts are balanced by body part.

Use Tracking Charts

Use the tracking charts included to help you plan and track your improvements.

Body Measurement Worksheet

Track your body improvements in the Body Measurement Worksheet (see page 32). Remember to measure yourself at the same time of day and at the same body points to get the most accurate comparisons. Set goals for improvements. Track your measurements every 30 days for the first six months of a program, and every 60 to 90 days afterward. Review your training when you record your measurements to understand why you're achieving the results you are and adjust your program as needed.

Progression Worksheet

Track your improvements in sets, reps, and weight for each exercise on the Progression Worksheet (see pages 33–34). Review your progress for each exercise in each body part. Be sure you're not focusing on one body part excessively while ignoring another body part. Enjoy entering these achievements and seeing your progress.

Body Measurement Worksheet

	Start	30 Days	60 Days	90 Days	120 Days
Date					
Height					
Body Weight					
Neck					
Right Upper Arm					
Left Upper Arm					
Right Forearm					
Left Forearm					
Chest					
Waist					
Hips					
Right Thigh					
Left Thigh					
Right Calf					
Left Calf					

Goals/Notes: _____

_____

_____

_____

Progression Worksheet

DATE:	Start Sets/Reps/Wt.	30 Days Sets/Reps/Wt.	60 Days Sets/Reps/Wt.	90 Days Sets/Reps/Wt.	120 Days Sets/Reps/Wt.
EXERCISE Back					
Chest					
Shoulders					
Abdominals					

Progression Worksheet

DATE:					
	Start Sets/Reps/Wt.	30 Days Sets/Reps/Wt.	60 Days Sets/Reps/Wt.	90 Days Sets/Reps/Wt.	120 Days Sets/Reps/Wt.
EXERCISE					
Biceps					
Triceps					
Upper Legs					
Lower Legs					

Training Diary

"A man is not old until regrets take the place of dreams."
—*John Barrymore*

DAY
1

○ MONDAY   ○ THURSDAY   ○ SUNDAY
○ TUESDAY   ○ FRIDAY
○ WEDNESDAY   ○ SATURDAY   _____
                                         Date

Warm-Up _____
_____

Body Focus/Exercise	SETS	REPS	WEIGHTS

Conditioning/Cardio _____
_____
_____
_____

Nutrition/Notes _____
_____

Feeling

○ **MONDAY**   ○ **THURSDAY**   ○ **SUNDAY**

○ **TUESDAY**   ○ **FRIDAY**

○ **WEDNESDAY**   ○ **SATURDAY**   _____

                                            Date

Warm-Up _____

_____

Body Focus/Exercise	SETS	REPS	WEIGHTS

Conditioning/Cardio _____

_____

_____

_____

Nutrition/Notes _____

_____

Feeling

DAY 3

○ **MONDAY**   ○ **THURSDAY**   ○ **SUNDAY**
○ **TUESDAY**   ○ **FRIDAY**
○ **WEDNESDAY**   ○ **SATURDAY**   _____
                                          Date

Warm-Up _____
_____

Body Focus/Exercise	SETS	REPS	WEIGHTS

Conditioning/Cardio _____
_____
_____
_____

Nutrition/Notes _____
_____

Feeling

DAY 4

○ **MONDAY**   ○ **THURSDAY**   ○ **SUNDAY**
○ **TUESDAY**   ○ **FRIDAY**
○ **WEDNESDAY**   ○ **SATURDAY**   _____
                                        Date

Warm-Up _____
_____

Body Focus/Exercise	SETS	REPS	WEIGHTS

Conditioning/Cardio _____
_____
_____
_____

Nutrition/Notes _____
_____

Feeling

DAY 5

○ MONDAY   ○ THURSDAY   ○ SUNDAY

○ TUESDAY   ○ FRIDAY

○ WEDNESDAY   ○ SATURDAY   _____

Date

Warm-Up _____

_____

Body Focus/Exercise	SETS	REPS	WEIGHTS

Conditioning/Cardio _____

_____

_____

_____

Nutrition/Notes _____

_____

Feeling   🙂   😐   🙁

○ **MONDAY**   ○ **THURSDAY**   ○ **SUNDAY**

○ **TUESDAY**   ○ **FRIDAY**

○ **WEDNESDAY**   ○ **SATURDAY**   _____

Date

Warm-Up _____

_____

Body Focus/Exercise	SETS	REPS	WEIGHTS

Conditioning/Cardio _____

_____

_____

_____

_____

Nutrition/Notes _____

_____

Feeling

DAY 7

○ MONDAY   ○ THURSDAY   ○ SUNDAY

○ TUESDAY   ○ FRIDAY

○ WEDNESDAY   ○ SATURDAY   _____

Date

Warm-Up _____

_____

Body Focus/Exercise	SETS	REPS	WEIGHTS

Conditioning/Cardio _____

_____

_____

_____

Nutrition/Notes _____

_____

Feeling

○ **MONDAY**   ○ **THURSDAY**   ○ **SUNDAY**

○ **TUESDAY**   ○ **FRIDAY**

○ **WEDNESDAY**   ○ **SATURDAY**   _____

Date

Warm-Up _____

_____

Body Focus/Exercise	SETS	REPS	WEIGHTS

Conditioning/Cardio _____

_____

_____

_____

Nutrition/Notes _____

_____

Feeling

DAY 9

○ **MONDAY**   ○ **THURSDAY**   ○ **SUNDAY**
○ **TUESDAY**   ○ **FRIDAY**
○ **WEDNESDAY** ○ **SATURDAY**   _____
                                          Date

Warm-Up _____
_____

Body Focus/Exercise	SETS	REPS	WEIGHTS

Conditioning/Cardio _____
_____
_____
_____

Nutrition/Notes _____
_____

Feeling

○ **MONDAY**   ○ **THURSDAY**   ○ **SUNDAY**

○ **TUESDAY**   ○ **FRIDAY**

○ **WEDNESDAY**   ○ **SATURDAY**   _____

Date

DAY

10

Warm-Up _____

_____

Body Focus/Exercise	SETS	REPS	WEIGHTS

Conditioning/Cardio _____

_____

_____

_____

_____

Nutrition/Notes _____

_____

Feeling   😐   🙂   ☺

DAY 11

○ MONDAY   ○ THURSDAY   ○ SUNDAY
○ TUESDAY   ○ FRIDAY
○ WEDNESDAY ○ SATURDAY

_____
Date

Warm-Up _____

_____

Body Focus/Exercise   SETS   REPS   WEIGHTS

_____   _____   _____   _____

_____   _____   _____   _____

_____   _____   _____   _____

_____   _____   _____   _____

_____   _____   _____   _____

_____   _____   _____   _____

_____   _____   _____   _____

_____   _____   _____   _____

_____   _____   _____   _____

_____   _____   _____   _____

_____   _____   _____   _____

_____   _____   _____   _____

_____   _____   _____   _____

_____   _____   _____   _____

_____   _____   _____   _____

_____   _____   _____   _____

_____   _____   _____   _____

_____   _____   _____   _____

Conditioning/Cardio _____

_____

_____

_____

_____

Nutrition/Notes _____

_____

Feeling   😕   😐   🙂

○ **MONDAY** ○ **THURSDAY** ○ **SUNDAY**
○ **TUESDAY** ○ **FRIDAY**
○ **WEDNESDAY** ○ **SATURDAY** _____

Date

DAY
12

Warm-Up _____
_____

Body Focus/Exercise	SETS	REPS	WEIGHTS
_____	_____	_____	_____
_____	_____	_____	_____
_____	_____	_____	_____
_____	_____	_____	_____
_____	_____	_____	_____
_____	_____	_____	_____
_____	_____	_____	_____
_____	_____	_____	_____
_____	_____	_____	_____
_____	_____	_____	_____
_____	_____	_____	_____
_____	_____	_____	_____
_____	_____	_____	_____
_____	_____	_____	_____
_____	_____	_____	_____
_____	_____	_____	_____
_____	_____	_____	_____

Conditioning/Cardio _____
_____
_____
_____

Nutrition/Notes _____
_____

Feeling

DAY 13

○ **MONDAY**　　○ **THURSDAY**　　○ **SUNDAY**
○ **TUESDAY**　　○ **FRIDAY**
○ **WEDNESDAY**　○ **SATURDAY**

_____
Date

Warm-Up _____

_____

Body Focus/Exercise	SETS	REPS	WEIGHTS

Conditioning/Cardio _____

_____

_____

_____

Nutrition/Notes _____

_____

Feeling

○ **MONDAY**　　○ **THURSDAY**　　○ **SUNDAY**

○ **TUESDAY**　　○ **FRIDAY**

○ **WEDNESDAY**　○ **SATURDAY**　_____

Date

DAY

14

Warm-Up _____

_____

Body Focus/Exercise	SETS	REPS	WEIGHTS

Conditioning/Cardio _____

_____

_____

_____

Nutrition/Notes _____

_____

Feeling

14-Day Review

_____ to _____
        Date   Date

Goals Met _____
_____
_____

WORKOUT SUMMARY

	No. of Workouts	No. of Exercises	(No. of Exercises by Body Part ÷ Total No. of Exercises)
Upper Body			
Back			
Chest			
Shoulders			
Abdominals			
Biceps			
Triceps			
Lower Body			
Upper Legs			
Lower Legs			
Cardio			
Cardio			
TOTAL			

BODY WEIGHT _____ _____ _____
                    Day 1   Day 7   Day 14

Feeling/Comments 😟 😐 🙂

_____

Goals for Next 14 Days _____

_____

"The first wealth is health." —**Emerson**

DAY
1

○ **MONDAY**　　○ **THURSDAY**　　○ **SUNDAY**
○ **TUESDAY**　　○ **FRIDAY**
○ **WEDNESDAY**　○ **SATURDAY**　　_____

Date

Warm-Up _____
_____

Body Focus/Exercise	SETS	REPS	WEIGHTS

Conditioning/Cardio _____
_____
_____
_____

Nutrition/Notes _____
_____

Feeling

○ **MONDAY**   ○ **THURSDAY**   ○ **SUNDAY**
○ **TUESDAY**   ○ **FRIDAY**
○ **WEDNESDAY**   ○ **SATURDAY**   _____
                                              Date

Warm-Up _____
_____

Body Focus/Exercise	SETS	REPS	WEIGHTS

Conditioning/Cardio _____
_____
_____
_____

Nutrition/Notes _____
_____

Feeling   ☺   ☺   ☺

DAY 3

○ **MONDAY**   ○ **THURSDAY**   ○ **SUNDAY**
○ **TUESDAY**   ○ **FRIDAY**
○ **WEDNESDAY**   ○ **SATURDAY**   _____
                                           Date

Warm-Up _____

_____

Body Focus/Exercise	SETS	REPS	WEIGHTS

Conditioning/Cardio _____

_____

_____

_____

Nutrition/Notes _____

_____

Feeling 😐 🙂 🙂

○ MONDAY ○ THURSDAY ○ SUNDAY
○ TUESDAY ○ FRIDAY
○ WEDNESDAY ○ SATURDAY _____

Date

Warm-Up _____

_____

Body Focus/Exercise	SETS	REPS	WEIGHTS

Conditioning/Cardio _____

_____

_____

_____

Nutrition/Notes _____

_____

Feeling

DAY 5

- ○ **MONDAY**
- ○ **TUESDAY**
- ○ **WEDNESDAY**
- ○ **THURSDAY**
- ○ **FRIDAY**
- ○ **SATURDAY**
- ○ **SUNDAY**

_____
Date

Warm-Up _____
_____

Body Focus/Exercise	SETS	REPS	WEIGHTS

Conditioning/Cardio _____
_____
_____
_____

Nutrition/Notes _____
_____

Feeling

○ **MONDAY**   ○ **THURSDAY**   ○ **SUNDAY**
○ **TUESDAY**   ○ **FRIDAY**
○ **WEDNESDAY**   ○ **SATURDAY**   _____

Date

Warm-Up _____

Body Focus/Exercise	SETS	REPS	WEIGHTS

Conditioning/Cardio _____

Nutrition/Notes _____

Feeling

DAY
7

○ MONDAY   ○ THURSDAY   ○ SUNDAY
○ TUESDAY   ○ FRIDAY
○ WEDNESDAY   ○ SATURDAY   _____
                                        Date

Warm-Up _____
_____

Body Focus/Exercise	SETS	REPS	WEIGHTS

Conditioning/Cardio _____
_____
_____
_____
_____

Nutrition/Notes _____
_____

Feeling

○ MONDAY   ○ THURSDAY   ○ SUNDAY

○ TUESDAY   ○ FRIDAY

○ WEDNESDAY   ○ SATURDAY

_____

Date

Warm-Up _____

_____

Body Focus/Exercise	SETS	REPS	WEIGHTS

Conditioning/Cardio _____

_____

_____

_____

Nutrition/Notes _____

_____

Feeling   ☹   😐   ☺

DAY
9

○ **MONDAY**   ○ **THURSDAY**   ○ **SUNDAY**
○ **TUESDAY**   ○ **FRIDAY**
○ **WEDNESDAY** ○ **SATURDAY**   _____
                                   Date

Warm-Up _____

_____

Body Focus/Exercise	SETS	REPS	WEIGHTS
_____	_____	_____	_____
_____	_____	_____	_____
_____	_____	_____	_____
_____	_____	_____	_____
_____	_____	_____	_____
_____	_____	_____	_____
_____	_____	_____	_____
_____	_____	_____	_____
_____	_____	_____	_____
_____	_____	_____	_____
_____	_____	_____	_____
_____	_____	_____	_____
_____	_____	_____	_____
_____	_____	_____	_____
_____	_____	_____	_____
_____	_____	_____	_____
_____	_____	_____	_____
_____	_____	_____	_____

Conditioning/Cardio _____

_____

_____

_____

Nutrition/Notes _____

_____

Feeling

○ **MONDAY**　　○ **THURSDAY**　　○ **SUNDAY**
○ **TUESDAY**　　○ **FRIDAY**
○ **WEDNESDAY**　○ **SATURDAY**　　_____

Date

Warm-Up _____

_____

Body Focus/Exercise	SETS	REPS	WEIGHTS

Conditioning/Cardio _____

_____

_____

_____

_____

Nutrition/Notes _____

_____

Feeling　　😐　　😐　　🙂

DAY
11

○ **MONDAY**   ○ **THURSDAY**   ○ **SUNDAY**
○ **TUESDAY**   ○ **FRIDAY**
○ **WEDNESDAY**   ○ **SATURDAY**   _____
                                       Date

Warm-Up _____

_____

Body Focus/Exercise	SETS	REPS	WEIGHTS

Conditioning/Cardio _____

_____

_____

_____

Nutrition/Notes _____

_____

Feeling

○ **MONDAY**   ○ **THURSDAY**   ○ **SUNDAY**
○ **TUESDAY**   ○ **FRIDAY**
○ **WEDNESDAY** ○ **SATURDAY**   _____

Date

DAY
12

Warm-Up _____

_____

Body Focus/Exercise	SETS	REPS	WEIGHTS

Conditioning/Cardio _____

_____

_____

_____

Nutrition/Notes _____

_____

Feeling

DAY 13

○ MONDAY ○ THURSDAY ○ SUNDAY
○ TUESDAY ○ FRIDAY
○ WEDNESDAY ○ SATURDAY _____
Date

Warm-Up _____

_____

Body Focus/Exercise	SETS	REPS	WEIGHTS

Conditioning/Cardio _____

_____

_____

_____

Nutrition/Notes _____

_____

Feeling

○ **MONDAY**   ○ **THURSDAY**   ○ **SUNDAY**
○ **TUESDAY**   ○ **FRIDAY**
○ **WEDNESDAY**   ○ **SATURDAY**   _____

Date

DAY
14

Warm-Up _____
_____

Body Focus/Exercise	SETS	REPS	WEIGHTS

Conditioning/Cardio _____
_____
_____
_____
_____

Nutrition/Notes _____
_____

Feeling

14-Day Review

_____ to _____
      Date   Date

Goals Met _____

_____

_____

WORKOUT SUMMARY

	No. of Workouts	No. of Exercises	(No. of Exercises by Body Part ÷ Total No. of Exercises)
Upper Body			
Back			
Chest			
Shoulders			
Abdominals			
Biceps			
Triceps			
Lower Body			
Upper Legs			
Lower Legs			
Cardio			
Cardio			
TOTAL			

BODY WEIGHT _____ _____ _____
                       Day 1   Day 7   Day 14

Feeling/Comments

_____

Goals for Next 14 Days _____

_____

*"I don't want to achieve immortality through my work.
I want to achieve it through not dying." —Woody Allen*

DAY 1

- ○ **MONDAY**
- ○ **TUESDAY**
- ○ **WEDNESDAY**
- ○ **THURSDAY**
- ○ **FRIDAY**
- ○ **SATURDAY**
- ○ **SUNDAY**

_____
Date

Warm-Up _____

_____

Body Focus/Exercise	SETS	REPS	WEIGHTS

Conditioning/Cardio _____

_____

_____

_____

Nutrition/Notes _____

_____

Feeling

○ **MONDAY**   ○ **THURSDAY**   ○ **SUNDAY**
○ **TUESDAY**   ○ **FRIDAY**
○ **WEDNESDAY** ○ **SATURDAY**   _____
                                          Date

Warm-Up _____

_____

Body Focus/Exercise	SETS	REPS	WEIGHTS

Conditioning/Cardio _____

_____

_____

_____

Nutrition/Notes _____

_____

Feeling

DAY 3

○ MONDAY   ○ THURSDAY   ○ SUNDAY
○ TUESDAY   ○ FRIDAY
○ WEDNESDAY   ○ SATURDAY   _____

Date

Warm-Up _____

_____

Body Focus/Exercise	SETS	REPS	WEIGHTS

Conditioning/Cardio _____

_____

_____

_____

Nutrition/Notes _____

_____

Feeling

○ MONDAY   ○ THURSDAY   ○ SUNDAY
○ TUESDAY   ○ FRIDAY
○ WEDNESDAY ○ SATURDAY   _____
                              Date

Warm-Up _____

_____

Body Focus/Exercise	SETS	REPS	WEIGHTS

Conditioning/Cardio _____

_____

_____

_____

Nutrition/Notes _____

_____

Feeling

DAY 5

○ MONDAY ○ THURSDAY ○ SUNDAY
○ TUESDAY ○ FRIDAY
○ WEDNESDAY ○ SATURDAY

_____
Date

Warm-Up _____

_____

Body Focus/Exercise	SETS	REPS	WEIGHTS

Conditioning/Cardio _____

_____

_____

_____

Nutrition/Notes _____

_____

Feeling

○ **MONDAY**   ○ **THURSDAY**   ○ **SUNDAY**
○ **TUESDAY**   ○ **FRIDAY**
○ **WEDNESDAY**   ○ **SATURDAY**   _____
                                          Date

Warm-Up _____
_____

Body Focus/Exercise	SETS	REPS	WEIGHTS

Conditioning/Cardio _____
_____
_____
_____
_____

Nutrition/Notes _____
_____

Feeling

DAY
7

○ MONDAY   ○ THURSDAY   ○ SUNDAY
○ TUESDAY   ○ FRIDAY
○ WEDNESDAY   ○ SATURDAY   _____

Date

Warm-Up _____

_____

Body Focus/Exercise	SETS	REPS	WEIGHTS

Conditioning/Cardio _____

_____

_____

_____

Nutrition/Notes _____

_____

Feeling

○ **MONDAY**   ○ **THURSDAY**   ○ **SUNDAY**

○ **TUESDAY**   ○ **FRIDAY**

○ **WEDNESDAY**   ○ **SATURDAY**   _____

Date

Warm-Up _____

_____

Body Focus/Exercise	SETS	REPS	WEIGHTS

Conditioning/Cardio _____

_____

_____

_____

Nutrition/Notes _____

_____

Feeling

DAY 9

○ MONDAY   ○ THURSDAY   ○ SUNDAY
○ TUESDAY   ○ FRIDAY
○ WEDNESDAY   ○ SATURDAY

_____
Date

Warm-Up _____
_____

Body Focus/Exercise	SETS	REPS	WEIGHTS

Conditioning/Cardio _____
_____
_____
_____

Nutrition/Notes _____
_____

Feeling

⚪ **MONDAY**　　⚪ **THURSDAY**　　⚪ **SUNDAY**

⚪ **TUESDAY**　　⚪ **FRIDAY**

⚪ **WEDNESDAY**　⚪ **SATURDAY**　　_____

Date

Warm-Up _____

_____

Body Focus/Exercise	SETS	REPS	WEIGHTS

Conditioning/Cardio _____

_____

_____

_____

Nutrition/Notes _____

_____

Feeling

DAY
11

○ **MONDAY**   ○ **THURSDAY**   ○ **SUNDAY**
○ **TUESDAY**   ○ **FRIDAY**
○ **WEDNESDAY**   ○ **SATURDAY**   _____
                                      Date

Warm-Up _____ . ____

_____

Body Focus/Exercise	SETS	REPS	WEIGHTS

Conditioning/Cardio _____

_____

_____

_____

_____

Nutrition/Notes _____

_____

Feeling

○ **MONDAY**   ○ **THURSDAY**   ○ **SUNDAY**

○ **TUESDAY**   ○ **FRIDAY**

○ **WEDNESDAY**   ○ **SATURDAY**   _____

Date

DAY

12

Warm-Up _____

_____

Body Focus/Exercise	SETS	REPS	WEIGHTS

Conditioning/Cardio _____

_____

_____

_____

Nutrition/Notes _____

_____

Feeling

DAY
13

○ MONDAY   ○ THURSDAY   ○ SUNDAY
○ TUESDAY   ○ FRIDAY
○ WEDNESDAY   ○ SATURDAY   _____
                                  Date

Warm-Up _____

_____

Body Focus/Exercise   SETS   REPS   WEIGHTS

_____   _____   _____   _____

_____   _____   _____   _____

_____   _____   _____   _____

_____   _____   _____   _____

_____   _____   _____   _____

_____   _____   _____   _____

_____   _____   _____   _____

_____   _____   _____   _____

_____   _____   _____   _____

_____   _____   _____   _____

_____   _____   _____   _____

_____   _____   _____   _____

_____   _____   _____   _____

_____   _____   _____   _____

_____   _____   _____   _____

_____   _____   _____   _____

_____   _____   _____   _____

_____   _____   _____   _____

Conditioning/Cardio _____

_____

_____

_____

Nutrition/Notes _____

_____

Feeling

○ **MONDAY**　　○ **THURSDAY**　　○ **SUNDAY**
○ **TUESDAY**　　○ **FRIDAY**
○ **WEDNESDAY**　○ **SATURDAY**　　_____

Date

Warm-Up _____

_____

Body Focus/Exercise	SETS	REPS	WEIGHTS

Conditioning/Cardio _____

_____

_____

_____

Nutrition/Notes _____

_____

Feeling

14-Day Review

_____ to _____
Date   Date

Goals Met _____

_____

_____

WORKOUT SUMMARY

	No. of Workouts	No. of Exercises	(No. of Exercises by Body Part ÷ Total No. of Exercises)
Upper Body			
Back			
Chest			
Shoulders			
Abdominals			
Biceps			
Triceps			
Lower Body			
Upper Legs			
Lower Legs			
Cardio			
Cardio			
TOTAL			

BODY WEIGHT   _____   _____   _____
                                  Day 1   Day 7   Day 14

Feeling/Comments   ☺   ☺   ☺

_____

Goals for Next 14 Days _____

_____

"Fitness: If it came in a bottle, everybody would have a great body." —Cher

DAY 1

○ **MONDAY**   ○ **THURSDAY**   ○ **SUNDAY**
○ **TUESDAY**   ○ **FRIDAY**
○ **WEDNESDAY**   ○ **SATURDAY**   _____
                                          Date

Warm-Up _____

_____

Body Focus/Exercise	SETS	REPS	WEIGHTS

Conditioning/Cardio _____

_____

_____

_____

Nutrition/Notes _____

_____

Feeling

○ **MONDAY**   ○ **THURSDAY**   ○ **SUNDAY**

○ **TUESDAY**   ○ **FRIDAY**

○ **WEDNESDAY**   ○ **SATURDAY**   _____

Date

Warm-Up _____

_____

Body Focus/Exercise	SETS	REPS	WEIGHTS

Conditioning/Cardio _____

_____

_____

_____

_____

Nutrition/Notes _____

_____

Feeling

DAY 3

○ **MONDAY**　　○ **THURSDAY**　　○ **SUNDAY**

○ **TUESDAY**　　○ **FRIDAY**

○ **WEDNESDAY**　○ **SATURDAY**　　_____

Date

Warm-Up _____

_____

Body Focus/Exercise	SETS	REPS	WEIGHTS

Conditioning/Cardio _____

_____

_____

_____

Nutrition/Notes _____

_____

Feeling

○ **MONDAY** ○ **THURSDAY** ○ **SUNDAY**
○ **TUESDAY** ○ **FRIDAY**
○ **WEDNESDAY** ○ **SATURDAY** _____

Date

DAY
4

Warm-Up _____

Body Focus/Exercise   SETS   REPS   WEIGHTS

_____   _____ _____ _____
_____   _____ _____ _____
_____   _____ _____ _____
_____   _____ _____ _____
_____   _____ _____ _____
_____   _____ _____ _____
_____   _____ _____ _____
_____   _____ _____ _____
_____   _____ _____ _____
_____   _____ _____ _____
_____   _____ _____ _____
_____   _____ _____ _____
_____   _____ _____ _____
_____   _____ _____ _____
_____   _____ _____ _____
_____   _____ _____ _____
_____   _____ _____ _____
_____   _____ _____ _____

Conditioning/Cardio _____

_____
_____
_____

Nutrition/Notes _____

_____

Feeling   😣   😐   🙂

DAY 5

○ **MONDAY**   ○ **THURSDAY**   ○ **SUNDAY**
○ **TUESDAY**   ○ **FRIDAY**
○ **WEDNESDAY**   ○ **SATURDAY**   _____
                                      Date

Warm-Up _____

_____

Body Focus/Exercise	SETS	REPS	WEIGHTS

Conditioning/Cardio _____

_____

_____

_____

Nutrition/Notes _____

_____

Feeling

○ **MONDAY**   ○ **THURSDAY**   ○ **SUNDAY**
○ **TUESDAY**   ○ **FRIDAY**
○ **WEDNESDAY** ○ **SATURDAY**   _____
                                        Date

DAY
6

Warm-Up _____

_____

Body Focus/Exercise	SETS	REPS	WEIGHTS

Conditioning/Cardio _____

_____

_____

_____

Nutrition/Notes _____

_____

Feeling

DAY
7

○ **MONDAY**   ○ **THURSDAY**   ○ **SUNDAY**
○ **TUESDAY**   ○ **FRIDAY**
○ **WEDNESDAY**   ○ **SATURDAY**   _____
                                        Date

Warm-Up _____

_____

Body Focus/Exercise	SETS	REPS	WEIGHTS

Conditioning/Cardio _____

_____

_____

_____

Nutrition/Notes _____

_____

Feeling

DAY 8

○ **MONDAY**   ○ **THURSDAY**   ○ **SUNDAY**
○ **TUESDAY**   ○ **FRIDAY**
○ **WEDNESDAY**   ○ **SATURDAY**   _____

Date

Warm-Up _____

_____

Body Focus/Exercise	SETS	REPS	WEIGHTS

Conditioning/Cardio _____

_____

_____

_____

Nutrition/Notes _____

_____

Feeling

DAY 9

- ○ **MONDAY**
- ○ **TUESDAY**
- ○ **WEDNESDAY**
- ○ **THURSDAY**
- ○ **FRIDAY**
- ○ **SATURDAY**
- ○ **SUNDAY**

_____
Date

Warm-Up _____
_____

Body Focus/Exercise	SETS	REPS	WEIGHTS

Conditioning/Cardio _____
_____
_____
_____

Nutrition/Notes _____
_____

Feeling 😐 🙂 😌

○ **MONDAY**   ○ **THURSDAY**   ○ **SUNDAY**

○ **TUESDAY**   ○ **FRIDAY**

○ **WEDNESDAY**   ○ **SATURDAY**   _____

Date

Warm-Up _____

_____

Body Focus/Exercise   SETS   REPS   WEIGHTS

_____   _____   _____   _____

_____   _____   _____   _____

_____   _____   _____   _____

_____   _____   _____   _____

_____   _____   _____   _____

_____   _____   _____   _____

_____   _____   _____   _____

_____   _____   _____   _____

_____   _____   _____   _____

_____   _____   _____   _____

_____   _____   _____   _____

_____   _____   _____   _____

_____   _____   _____   _____

_____   _____   _____   _____

_____   _____   _____   _____

_____   _____   _____   _____

_____   _____   _____   _____

Conditioning/Cardio _____

_____

_____

_____

_____

Nutrition/Notes _____

_____

Feeling   😕   😐   🙂

DAY
11

- ○ **MONDAY**
- ○ **TUESDAY**
- ○ **WEDNESDAY**
- ○ **THURSDAY**
- ○ **FRIDAY**
- ○ **SATURDAY**
- ○ **SUNDAY**

_____
Date

Warm-Up _____
_____

Body Focus/Exercise	SETS	REPS	WEIGHTS

Conditioning/Cardio _____
_____
_____
_____

Nutrition/Notes _____
_____

Feeling

○ **MONDAY**   ○ **THURSDAY**   ○ **SUNDAY**
○ **TUESDAY**   ○ **FRIDAY**
○ **WEDNESDAY**   ○ **SATURDAY**   _____
                                                Date

Warm-Up _____
_____

Body Focus/Exercise	SETS	REPS	WEIGHTS
_____	_____	_____	_____
_____	_____	_____	_____
_____	_____	_____	_____
_____	_____	_____	_____
_____	_____	_____	_____
_____	_____	_____	_____
_____	_____	_____	_____
_____	_____	_____	_____
_____	_____	_____	_____
_____	_____	_____	_____
_____	_____	_____	_____
_____	_____	_____	_____
_____	_____	_____	_____
_____	_____	_____	_____
_____	_____	_____	_____
_____	_____	_____	_____
_____	_____	_____	_____
_____	_____	_____	_____

Conditioning/Cardio _____
_____
_____
_____

Nutrition/Notes _____
_____

Feeling

DAY
13

○ MONDAY   ○ THURSDAY   ○ SUNDAY
○ TUESDAY   ○ FRIDAY
○ WEDNESDAY   ○ SATURDAY   _____
                                      Date

Warm-Up _____
_____

Body Focus/Exercise	SETS	REPS	WEIGHTS

Conditioning/Cardio _____
_____
_____
_____

Nutrition/Notes _____
_____

Feeling

○ **MONDAY**   ○ **THURSDAY**   ○ **SUNDAY**
○ **TUESDAY**   ○ **FRIDAY**
○ **WEDNESDAY**   ○ **SATURDAY**   _____
Date

Warm-Up _____

Body Focus/Exercise	SETS	REPS	WEIGHTS

Conditioning/Cardio _____

Nutrition/Notes _____

Feeling

14-Day Review

_____ to _____
      Date   Date

Goals Met _____

_____

_____

WORKOUT SUMMARY

	No. of Workouts	No. of Exercises	(No. of Exercises by Body Part ÷ Total No. of Exercises)
Upper Body			
Back			
Chest			
Shoulders			
Abdominals			
Biceps			
Triceps			
Lower Body			
Upper Legs			
Lower Legs			
Cardio			
Cardio			
TOTAL			

BODY WEIGHT   _____   _____   _____
                           Day 1   Day 7   Day 14

Feeling/Comments

_____

Goals for Next 14 Days _____

_____

"*Strength pilgrimage: The lazy never started and the weak died along the way.*" —Unknown

DAY 1

○ **MONDAY**　　○ **THURSDAY**　　○ **SUNDAY**
○ **TUESDAY**　　○ **FRIDAY**
○ **WEDNESDAY**　○ **SATURDAY**　　_____
　　　　　　　　　　　　　　　　　　　　　　　Date

Warm-Up _____
_____

Body Focus/Exercise	SETS	REPS	WEIGHTS

Conditioning/Cardio _____
_____
_____
_____

Nutrition/Notes _____
_____

Feeling

○ **MONDAY** ○ **THURSDAY** ○ **SUNDAY**
○ **TUESDAY** ○ **FRIDAY**
○ **WEDNESDAY** ○ **SATURDAY** _____
Date

DAY

2

Warm-Up _____

_____

Body Focus/Exercise	SETS	REPS	WEIGHTS

Conditioning/Cardio _____

_____

_____

_____

_____

Nutrition/Notes _____

_____

Feeling

DAY 3

○ **MONDAY**   ○ **THURSDAY**   ○ **SUNDAY**
○ **TUESDAY**   ○ **FRIDAY**
○ **WEDNESDAY**   ○ **SATURDAY**   _____
                                        Date

Warm-Up _____
_____

Body Focus/Exercise	SETS	REPS	WEIGHTS

Conditioning/Cardio _____
_____
_____
_____

Nutrition/Notes _____
_____

Feeling

○ **MONDAY**   ○ **THURSDAY**   ○ **SUNDAY**
○ **TUESDAY**   ○ **FRIDAY**
○ **WEDNESDAY**   ○ **SATURDAY** _____

Date

DAY
4

Warm-Up _____
_____

Body Focus/Exercise	SETS	REPS	WEIGHTS

Conditioning/Cardio _____
_____
_____
_____
_____

Nutrition/Notes _____
_____

Feeling

DAY 5

○ MONDAY   ○ THURSDAY   ○ SUNDAY
○ TUESDAY   ○ FRIDAY
○ WEDNESDAY   ○ SATURDAY   _____

Date

Warm-Up _____

_____

Body Focus/Exercise	SETS	REPS	WEIGHTS

Conditioning/Cardio _____

_____

_____

_____

Nutrition/Notes _____

_____

Feeling

DAY

6

○ **MONDAY**   ○ **THURSDAY**   ○ **SUNDAY**
○ **TUESDAY**   ○ **FRIDAY**
○ **WEDNESDAY**   ○ **SATURDAY**   _____

Date

Warm-Up _____

_____

Body Focus/Exercise	SETS	REPS	WEIGHTS

Conditioning/Cardio _____

_____

_____

_____

Nutrition/Notes _____

_____

Feeling

DAY 7

○ MONDAY   ○ THURSDAY   ○ SUNDAY
○ TUESDAY   ○ FRIDAY
○ WEDNESDAY   ○ SATURDAY   _____
                                   Date

Warm-Up _____

Body Focus/Exercise   SETS   REPS   WEIGHTS

_____   _____   _____   _____
_____   _____   _____   _____
_____   _____   _____   _____
_____   _____   _____   _____
_____   _____   _____   _____
_____   _____   _____   _____
_____   _____   _____   _____
_____   _____   _____   _____
_____   _____   _____   _____
_____   _____   _____   _____
_____   _____   _____   _____
_____   _____   _____   _____
_____   _____   _____   _____
_____   _____   _____   _____
_____   _____   _____   _____
_____   _____   _____   _____
_____   _____   _____   _____
_____   _____   _____   _____

Conditioning/Cardio _____
_____
_____
_____

Nutrition/Notes _____
_____

Feeling   😐   😑   🙂

○ **MONDAY** ○ **THURSDAY** ○ **SUNDAY**
○ **TUESDAY** ○ **FRIDAY**
○ **WEDNESDAY** ○ **SATURDAY** _____
Date

Warm-Up _____
_____

Body Focus/Exercise	SETS	REPS	WEIGHTS

Conditioning/Cardio _____
_____
_____
_____
_____

Nutrition/Notes _____
_____

Feeling

DAY
9

○ **MONDAY**   ○ **THURSDAY**   ○ **SUNDAY**
○ **TUESDAY**   ○ **FRIDAY**
○ **WEDNESDAY**   ○ **SATURDAY**   _____
                                         Date

Warm-Up _____

_____

Body Focus/Exercise	SETS	REPS	WEIGHTS

Conditioning/Cardio _____

_____

_____

_____

Nutrition/Notes _____

_____

Feeling

DAY 10

○ **MONDAY**   ○ **THURSDAY**   ○ **SUNDAY**
○ **TUESDAY**   ○ **FRIDAY**
○ **WEDNESDAY**   ○ **SATURDAY**   _____
                                       Date

Warm-Up _____
_____

Body Focus/Exercise	SETS	REPS	WEIGHTS

Conditioning/Cardio _____
_____
_____
_____

Nutrition/Notes _____
_____

Feeling 😐 😐 😐

DAY
11

○ MONDAY   ○ THURSDAY   ○ SUNDAY
○ TUESDAY   ○ FRIDAY
○ WEDNESDAY   ○ SATURDAY   _____
                                            Date

Warm-Up _____

_____

Body Focus/Exercise   SETS   REPS   WEIGHTS

_____   _____   _____   _____

_____   _____   _____   _____

_____   _____   _____   _____

_____   _____   _____   _____

_____   _____   _____   _____

_____   _____   _____   _____

_____   _____   _____   _____

_____   _____   _____   _____

_____   _____   _____   _____

_____   _____   _____   _____

_____   _____   _____   _____

_____   _____   _____   _____

_____   _____   _____   _____

_____   _____   _____   _____

_____   _____   _____   _____

_____   _____   _____   _____

_____   _____   _____   _____

_____   _____   _____   _____

Conditioning/Cardio _____

_____

_____

_____

Nutrition/Notes _____

_____

Feeling

○ **MONDAY**　　○ **THURSDAY**　　○ **SUNDAY**

○ **TUESDAY**　　○ **FRIDAY**

○ **WEDNESDAY**　○ **SATURDAY**　　_____

　　　　　　　　　　　　　　　　　　Date

Warm-Up _____

_____

Body Focus/Exercise	SETS	REPS	WEIGHTS

Conditioning/Cardio _____

_____

_____

_____

_____

Nutrition/Notes _____

_____

Feeling

DAY 13

2

○ MONDAY   ○ THURSDAY   ○ SUNDAY
○ TUESDAY   ○ FRIDAY
○ WEDNESDAY   ○ SATURDAY   _____
                                        Date

Warm-Up _____

_____

Body Focus/Exercise	SETS	REPS	WEIGHTS

Conditioning/Cardio _____

_____

_____

_____

Nutrition/Notes _____

_____

Feeling

DAY
14

○ **MONDAY**   ○ **THURSDAY**   ○ **SUNDAY**
○ **TUESDAY**   ○ **FRIDAY**
○ **WEDNESDAY** ○ **SATURDAY**   _____
                                  Date

Warm-Up _____
_____

Body Focus/Exercise	SETS	REPS	WEIGHTS

Conditioning/Cardio _____
_____
_____
_____

Nutrition/Notes _____
_____

Feeling   ☹   😐   ☺

14-Day Review

_____ **to** _____
　　Date　　　　　　　　　Date

Goals Met _____

_____

_____

WORKOUT SUMMARY

	No. of Workouts	No. of Exercises	(No. of Exercises by Body Part ÷ Total No. of Exercises)
Upper Body			
Back			
Chest			
Shoulders			
Abdominals			
Biceps			
Triceps			
Lower Body			
Upper Legs			
Lower Legs			
Cardio			
Cardio			
TOTAL			

BODY WEIGHT　_____　_____　_____
　　　　　　　　　　　　Day 1　　　　　　　　Day 7　　　　　　　Day 14

Feeling/Comments　😕　😐　🙂

_____

Goals for Next 14 Days _____

_____

"Failure is the path of least persistence." —*Unknown*

DAY 1

○ MONDAY ○ THURSDAY ○ SUNDAY
○ TUESDAY ○ FRIDAY
○ WEDNESDAY ○ SATURDAY _____

Date

Warm-Up _____

_____

Body Focus/Exercise	SETS	REPS	WEIGHTS

Conditioning/Cardio _____

_____

_____

_____

Nutrition/Notes _____

_____

Feeling

DAY 2

○ **MONDAY**　　○ **THURSDAY**　　○ **SUNDAY**
○ **TUESDAY**　　○ **FRIDAY**
○ **WEDNESDAY**　○ **SATURDAY**　　_____

Date

Warm-Up _____

_____

Body Focus/Exercise	SETS	REPS	WEIGHTS

Conditioning/Cardio _____

_____

_____

_____

_____

Nutrition/Notes _____

_____

Feeling

DAY
3

○ MONDAY   ○ THURSDAY   ○ SUNDAY
○ TUESDAY   ○ FRIDAY
○ WEDNESDAY   ○ SATURDAY   _____
                              Date

Warm-Up _____

_____

Body Focus/Exercise	SETS	REPS	WEIGHTS

Conditioning/Cardio _____

_____

_____

_____

Nutrition/Notes _____

_____

Feeling

○ **MONDAY** ○ **THURSDAY** ○ **SUNDAY**
○ **TUESDAY** ○ **FRIDAY**
○ **WEDNESDAY** ○ **SATURDAY** _____

Date

DAY
4

Warm-Up _____

Body Focus/Exercise   SETS   REPS   WEIGHTS

_____   _____   _____   _____
_____   _____   _____   _____
_____   _____   _____   _____
_____   _____   _____   _____
_____   _____   _____   _____
_____   _____   _____   _____
_____   _____   _____   _____
_____   _____   _____   _____
_____   _____   _____   _____
_____   _____   _____   _____
_____   _____   _____   _____
_____   _____   _____   _____
_____   _____   _____   _____
_____   _____   _____   _____
_____   _____   _____   _____
_____   _____   _____   _____
_____   _____   _____   _____
_____   _____   _____   _____

Conditioning/Cardio _____

Nutrition/Notes _____

Feeling

DAY 5

○ **MONDAY**   ○ **THURSDAY**   ○ **SUNDAY**
○ **TUESDAY**   ○ **FRIDAY**
○ **WEDNESDAY**   ○ **SATURDAY**   _____
                                      Date

Warm-Up _____
_____

Body Focus/Exercise	SETS	REPS	WEIGHTS

Conditioning/Cardio _____
_____
_____
_____

Nutrition/Notes _____
_____

Feeling

○ **MONDAY**   ○ **THURSDAY**   ○ **SUNDAY**
○ **TUESDAY**   ○ **FRIDAY**
○ **WEDNESDAY**   ○ **SATURDAY**   _____
                                         Date

Warm-Up _____

_____

Body Focus/Exercise	SETS	REPS	WEIGHTS

Conditioning/Cardio _____

_____

_____

_____

_____

Nutrition/Notes _____

_____

Feeling   ☹   😐   ☺

DAY
7

○ **MONDAY**   ○ **THURSDAY**   ○ **SUNDAY**
○ **TUESDAY**   ○ **FRIDAY**
○ **WEDNESDAY**   ○ **SATURDAY**   _____
                                      Date

Warm-Up _____
_____

Body Focus/Exercise	SETS	REPS	WEIGHTS

Conditioning/Cardio _____
_____
_____
_____

Nutrition/Notes _____
_____

Feeling   ☺   ☺   ☺

○ MONDAY   ○ THURSDAY   ○ SUNDAY
○ TUESDAY   ○ FRIDAY
○ WEDNESDAY ○ SATURDAY   _____

Date

Warm-Up _____
_____

Body Focus/Exercise	SETS	REPS	WEIGHTS

Conditioning/Cardio _____
_____
_____
_____

Nutrition/Notes _____
_____

Feeling   ☹   😐   ☺

DAY 9

○ **MONDAY**   ○ **THURSDAY**   ○ **SUNDAY**
○ **TUESDAY**   ○ **FRIDAY**
○ **WEDNESDAY**   ○ **SATURDAY**   _____
                                         Date

Warm-Up _____
_____

Body Focus/Exercise	SETS	REPS	WEIGHTS

Conditioning/Cardio _____
_____
_____
_____

Nutrition/Notes _____
_____

Feeling

○ **MONDAY**   ○ **THURSDAY**   ○ **SUNDAY**
○ **TUESDAY**   ○ **FRIDAY**
○ **WEDNESDAY**   ○ **SATURDAY**   _____
                                              Date

DAY
10

Warm-Up _____
_____

Body Focus/Exercise	SETS	REPS	WEIGHTS

Conditioning/Cardio _____
_____
_____
_____

Nutrition/Notes _____
_____

Feeling

DAY 11

○ **MONDAY**   ○ **THURSDAY**   ○ **SUNDAY**
○ **TUESDAY**   ○ **FRIDAY**
○ **WEDNESDAY**   ○ **SATURDAY**   _____
Date

Warm-Up _____
_____

Body Focus/Exercise	SETS	REPS	WEIGHTS

Conditioning/Cardio _____
_____
_____
_____

Nutrition/Notes _____
_____

Feeling   ☹   😐   ☺

○ **MONDAY**   ○ **THURSDAY**   ○ **SUNDAY**
○ **TUESDAY**   ○ **FRIDAY**
○ **WEDNESDAY** ○ **SATURDAY**   _____
                                   Date

DAY
12

Warm-Up _____

_____

Body Focus/Exercise	SETS	REPS	WEIGHTS

Conditioning/Cardio _____

_____

_____

_____

Nutrition/Notes _____

_____

Feeling

DAY 13

○ **MONDAY**　　○ **THURSDAY**　　○ **SUNDAY**
○ **TUESDAY**　　○ **FRIDAY**
○ **WEDNESDAY**　○ **SATURDAY**　　_____
　　　　　　　　　　　　　　　　　　　　　Date

Warm-Up _____

_____

Body Focus/Exercise	SETS	REPS	WEIGHTS

Conditioning/Cardio _____

_____

_____

_____

_____

Nutrition/Notes _____

_____

Feeling

○ **MONDAY** ○ **THURSDAY** ○ **SUNDAY**
○ **TUESDAY** ○ **FRIDAY**
○ **WEDNESDAY** ○ **SATURDAY** _____

Date

Warm-Up _____

_____

Body Focus/Exercise	SETS	REPS	WEIGHTS

Conditioning/Cardio _____

_____

_____

_____

Nutrition/Notes _____

_____

Feeling 😐 😐 😊

14-Day Review

_____ to _____
     Date   Date

Goals Met _____

_____

_____

WORKOUT SUMMARY

	No. of Workouts	No. of Exercises	(No. of Exercises by Body Part ÷ Total No. of Exercises)
Upper Body			
Back			
Chest			
Shoulders			
Abdominals			
Biceps			
Triceps			
Lower Body			
Upper Legs			
Lower Legs			
Cardio			
Cardio			
TOTAL			

BODY WEIGHT   _____   _____   _____
                           Day 1   Day 7   Day 14

Feeling/Comments

_____

Goals for Next 14 Days _____

_____

"Happiness is nothing more than good health and a bad memory." —Albert Schweitzer

DAY 1

○ **MONDAY**   ○ **THURSDAY**   ○ **SUNDAY**
○ **TUESDAY**   ○ **FRIDAY**
○ **WEDNESDAY**   ○ **SATURDAY**   _____
                                            Date

Warm-Up _____
_____

Body Focus/Exercise	SETS	REPS	WEIGHTS

Conditioning/Cardio _____
_____
_____
_____

Nutrition/Notes _____
_____

Feeling

○ **MONDAY** ○ **THURSDAY** ○ **SUNDAY**
○ **TUESDAY** ○ **FRIDAY**
○ **WEDNESDAY** ○ **SATURDAY** _____
Date

DAY
2

Warm-Up _____
_____

Body Focus/Exercise	SETS	REPS	WEIGHTS

Conditioning/Cardio _____
_____
_____
_____

Nutrition/Notes _____
_____

Feeling

DAY 3

○ MONDAY   ○ THURSDAY   ○ SUNDAY
○ TUESDAY   ○ FRIDAY
○ WEDNESDAY   ○ SATURDAY   _____
                              Date

Warm-Up _____
_____

Body Focus/Exercise	SETS	REPS	WEIGHTS

Conditioning/Cardio _____
_____
_____
_____

Nutrition/Notes _____
_____

Feeling

○ **MONDAY**   ○ **THURSDAY**   ○ **SUNDAY**

○ **TUESDAY**   ○ **FRIDAY**

○ **WEDNESDAY**   ○ **SATURDAY**   _____

Date

DAY

4

Warm-Up _____

_____

Body Focus/Exercise	SETS	REPS	WEIGHTS

Conditioning/Cardio _____

_____

_____

_____

Nutrition/Notes _____

_____

Feeling   ☹   😐   🙂

DAY
5

○ MONDAY   ○ THURSDAY   ○ SUNDAY
○ TUESDAY   ○ FRIDAY
○ WEDNESDAY   ○ SATURDAY   _____

Date

Warm-Up _____

_____

Body Focus/Exercise	SETS	REPS	WEIGHTS

Conditioning/Cardio _____

_____

_____

_____

Nutrition/Notes _____

_____

Feeling

○ **MONDAY**   ○ **THURSDAY**   ○ **SUNDAY**
○ **TUESDAY**   ○ **FRIDAY**
○ **WEDNESDAY** ○ **SATURDAY**   _____

Date

Warm-Up _____

_____

Body Focus/Exercise	SETS	REPS	WEIGHTS

Conditioning/Cardio _____

_____

_____

_____

Nutrition/Notes _____

_____

Feeling

DAY 7

○ **MONDAY**   ○ **THURSDAY**   ○ **SUNDAY**
○ **TUESDAY**   ○ **FRIDAY**
○ **WEDNESDAY**   ○ **SATURDAY**   _____
                                        Date

Warm-Up _____
_____

Body Focus/Exercise	SETS	REPS	WEIGHTS

Conditioning/Cardio _____
_____
_____
_____

Nutrition/Notes _____
_____

Feeling

○ **MONDAY**   ○ **THURSDAY**   ○ **SUNDAY**

○ **TUESDAY**   ○ **FRIDAY**

○ **WEDNESDAY** ○ **SATURDAY**   _____

Date

Warm-Up _____

_____

Body Focus/Exercise	SETS	REPS	WEIGHTS

Conditioning/Cardio _____

_____

_____

_____

Nutrition/Notes _____

_____

Feeling

DAY 9

○ **MONDAY**   ○ **THURSDAY**   ○ **SUNDAY**
○ **TUESDAY**   ○ **FRIDAY**
○ **WEDNESDAY**   ○ **SATURDAY**   _____
                                      Date

Warm-Up _____
_____

Body Focus/Exercise	SETS	REPS	WEIGHTS

Conditioning/Cardio _____
_____
_____
_____

Nutrition/Notes _____
_____

Feeling   ☺   ☺   ☺

○ **MONDAY**   ○ **THURSDAY**   ○ **SUNDAY**

○ **TUESDAY**   ○ **FRIDAY**

○ **WEDNESDAY**   ○ **SATURDAY**   _____

Date

Warm-Up _____

_____

Body Focus/Exercise	SETS	REPS	WEIGHTS

Conditioning/Cardio _____

_____

_____

_____

_____

Nutrition/Notes _____

_____

Feeling

DAY 11

○ **MONDAY** ○ **THURSDAY** ○ **SUNDAY**
○ **TUESDAY** ○ **FRIDAY**
○ **WEDNESDAY** ○ **SATURDAY** _____
Date

Warm-Up _____

_____

Body Focus/Exercise	SETS	REPS	WEIGHTS

Conditioning/Cardio _____

_____

_____

_____

Nutrition/Notes _____

_____

Feeling

○ **MONDAY**   ○ **THURSDAY**   ○ **SUNDAY**

○ **TUESDAY**   ○ **FRIDAY**

○ **WEDNESDAY**   ○ **SATURDAY**   _____

Date

Warm-Up _____

_____

Body Focus/Exercise	SETS	REPS	WEIGHTS

Conditioning/Cardio _____

_____

_____

_____

Nutrition/Notes _____

_____

Feeling

DAY
13

Warm-Up _____
_____

Body Focus/Exercise	SETS	REPS	WEIGHTS

Conditioning/Cardio _____
_____
_____
_____
_____

Nutrition/Notes _____
_____

Feeling   😟   😐   🙂

○ **MONDAY**   ○ **THURSDAY**   ○ **SUNDAY**

○ **TUESDAY**   ○ **FRIDAY**

○ **WEDNESDAY**   ○ **SATURDAY**   _____

Date

DAY
14

Warm-Up _____

_____

Body Focus/Exercise	SETS	REPS	WEIGHTS

Conditioning/Cardio _____

_____

_____

_____

Nutrition/Notes _____

_____

Feeling   😕   🙂   😊

14-Day Review

_____ to _____
        Date   Date

Goals Met _____

_____

_____

WORKOUT SUMMARY

	No. of Workouts	No. of Exercises	(No. of Exercises by Body Part ÷ Total No. of Exercises)
Upper Body			
Back			
Chest			
Shoulders			
Abdominals			
Biceps			
Triceps			
Lower Body			
Upper Legs			
Lower Legs			
Cardio			
Cardio			
TOTAL			

BODY WEIGHT   _____   _____   _____
                        Day 1   Day 7   Day 14

Feeling/Comments

_____

Goals for Next 14 Days _____

_____

"Old age comes at a bad time." —*Unknown*

DAY 1

○ **MONDAY**   ○ **THURSDAY**   ○ **SUNDAY**
○ **TUESDAY**   ○ **FRIDAY**
○ **WEDNESDAY**   ○ **SATURDAY**   _____
                                         Date

Warm-Up _____

_____

Body Focus/Exercise	SETS	REPS	WEIGHTS

Conditioning/Cardio _____

_____

_____

_____

Nutrition/Notes _____

_____

Feeling

DAY 2

○ **MONDAY**   ○ **THURSDAY**   ○ **SUNDAY**
○ **TUESDAY**   ○ **FRIDAY**
○ **WEDNESDAY** ○ **SATURDAY**   _____
                                      Date

Warm-Up _____
_____

Body Focus/Exercise	SETS	REPS	WEIGHTS

Conditioning/Cardio _____
_____
_____
_____
_____

Nutrition/Notes _____
_____

Feeling   😕   😐   🙂

DAY 3

○ MONDAY   ○ THURSDAY   ○ SUNDAY
○ TUESDAY   ○ FRIDAY
○ WEDNESDAY ○ SATURDAY   _____

Date

Warm-Up _____

_____

Body Focus/Exercise	SETS	REPS	WEIGHTS

Conditioning/Cardio _____

_____

_____

_____

Nutrition/Notes _____

_____

Feeling

○ **MONDAY**   ○ **THURSDAY**   ○ **SUNDAY**
○ **TUESDAY**   ○ **FRIDAY**
○ **WEDNESDAY** ○ **SATURDAY**   _____
                                         Date

DAY
4

Warm-Up _____

_____

Body Focus/Exercise	SETS	REPS	WEIGHTS

Conditioning/Cardio _____

_____

_____

_____

Nutrition/Notes _____

_____

Feeling

DAY 5

○ **MONDAY** ○ **THURSDAY** ○ **SUNDAY**
○ **TUESDAY** ○ **FRIDAY**
○ **WEDNESDAY** ○ **SATURDAY**

_____
Date

Warm-Up _____
_____

Body Focus/Exercise	SETS	REPS	WEIGHTS

Conditioning/Cardio _____
_____
_____
_____

Nutrition/Notes _____
_____

Feeling

DAY
6

○ MONDAY   ○ THURSDAY   ○ SUNDAY
○ TUESDAY   ○ FRIDAY
○ WEDNESDAY ○ SATURDAY   _____
                                    Date

Warm-Up _____
_____

Body Focus/Exercise	SETS	REPS	WEIGHTS

Conditioning/Cardio _____
_____
_____
_____

Nutrition/Notes _____
_____

Feeling ☹ 😐 🙂

DAY 7

○ MONDAY   ○ THURSDAY   ○ SUNDAY
○ TUESDAY   ○ FRIDAY
○ WEDNESDAY   ○ SATURDAY   _____
                                      Date

Warm-Up _____
_____

Body Focus/Exercise   SETS   REPS   WEIGHTS

_____   _____   _____   _____
_____   _____   _____   _____
_____   _____   _____   _____
_____   _____   _____   _____
_____   _____   _____   _____
_____   _____   _____   _____
_____   _____   _____   _____
_____   _____   _____   _____
_____   _____   _____   _____
_____   _____   _____   _____
_____   _____   _____   _____
_____   _____   _____   _____
_____   _____   _____   _____
_____   _____   _____   _____
_____   _____   _____   _____
_____   _____   _____   _____
_____   _____   _____   _____
_____   _____   _____   _____
_____   _____   _____   _____

Conditioning/Cardio _____
_____
_____
_____

Nutrition/Notes _____
_____

Feeling   ☹   😐   🙂

○ **MONDAY** ○ **THURSDAY** ○ **SUNDAY**
○ **TUESDAY** ○ **FRIDAY**
○ **WEDNESDAY** ○ **SATURDAY** _____

Date

Warm-Up _____

_____

Body Focus/Exercise	SETS	REPS	WEIGHTS

Conditioning/Cardio _____

_____

_____

_____

Nutrition/Notes _____

_____

Feeling

DAY 9

○ **MONDAY**   ○ **THURSDAY**   ○ **SUNDAY**
○ **TUESDAY**   ○ **FRIDAY**
○ **WEDNESDAY**   ○ **SATURDAY**   _____
                                          Date

Warm-Up _____
_____

Body Focus/Exercise   SETS   REPS   WEIGHTS

_____   _____   _____   _____
_____   _____   _____   _____
_____   _____   _____   _____
_____   _____   _____   _____
_____   _____   _____   _____
_____   _____   _____   _____
_____   _____   _____   _____
_____   _____   _____   _____
_____   _____   _____   _____
_____   _____   _____   _____
_____   _____   _____   _____
_____   _____   _____   _____
_____   _____   _____   _____
_____   _____   _____   _____
_____   _____   _____   _____
_____   _____   _____   _____
_____   _____   _____   _____
_____   _____   _____   _____
_____   _____   _____   _____
_____   _____   _____   _____

Conditioning/Cardio _____
_____
_____
_____
_____

Nutrition/Notes _____
_____

Feeling

○ **MONDAY** ○ **THURSDAY** ○ **SUNDAY**
○ **TUESDAY** ○ **FRIDAY**
○ **WEDNESDAY** ○ **SATURDAY** _____

Date

Warm-Up _____
_____

Body Focus/Exercise	SETS	REPS	WEIGHTS

Conditioning/Cardio _____
_____
_____
_____
_____

Nutrition/Notes _____
_____

Feeling

DAY 11

○ **MONDAY**   ○ **THURSDAY**   ○ **SUNDAY**
○ **TUESDAY**   ○ **FRIDAY**
○ **WEDNESDAY**   ○ **SATURDAY**   _____

Date

Warm-Up _____

_____

Body Focus/Exercise	SETS	REPS	WEIGHTS

Conditioning/Cardio _____

_____

_____

_____

Nutrition/Notes _____

_____

Feeling

○ **MONDAY**   ○ **THURSDAY**   ○ **SUNDAY**
○ **TUESDAY**   ○ **FRIDAY**
○ **WEDNESDAY**   ○ **SATURDAY**   _____
                                           Date

Warm-Up _____
_____

Body Focus/Exercise	SETS	REPS	WEIGHTS

Conditioning/Cardio _____
_____
_____
_____

Nutrition/Notes _____
_____

Feeling   😟   😐   🙂

DAY
13

○ **MONDAY**　　○ **THURSDAY**　　○ **SUNDAY**

○ **TUESDAY**　　○ **FRIDAY**

○ **WEDNESDAY**　○ **SATURDAY**

_____
Date

Warm-Up _____

_____

Body Focus/Exercise	SETS	REPS	WEIGHTS

Conditioning/Cardio _____

_____

_____

_____

Nutrition/Notes _____

_____

Feeling

○ **MONDAY**   ○ **THURSDAY**   ○ **SUNDAY**
○ **TUESDAY**   ○ **FRIDAY**
○ **WEDNESDAY** ○ **SATURDAY**   _____
                                          Date

Warm-Up _____

_____

Body Focus/Exercise	SETS	REPS	WEIGHTS

Conditioning/Cardio _____

_____

_____

_____

Nutrition/Notes _____

_____

Feeling   😞   😐   🙂

14-Day Review

_____ to _____
Date   Date

Goals Met _____

_____

_____

WORKOUT SUMMARY

	No. of Workouts	No. of Exercises	(No. of Exercises by Body Part ÷ Total No. of Exercises)
Upper Body			
Back			
Chest			
Shoulders			
Abdominals			
Biceps			
Triceps			
Lower Body			
Upper Legs			
Lower Legs			
Cardio			
Cardio			
TOTAL			

BODY WEIGHT _____ _____ _____
Day 1   Day 7   Day 14

Feeling/Comments

_____

Goals for Next 14 Days _____

_____

Additional Resources

This training guide offers an introductory level of tips and workouts to help you get more out of your strength training. Consider the following excellent resources for more in-depth discussions of strength training and nutrition.

Books

The books in the following lists are great resources on the subjects of strength training and fitness nutrition.

Strength Training

Antonio, Jose. *Supplements for Strength-Power Athletes.* 2nd ed. Champaign, IL: Human Kinetics, 2002.

Baechle, Thomas R., and Barney R. Groves. *Weight Training.* Champaign, IL: Human Kinetics, 1998.

Bompa, Tudor. *Serious Strength Training.* 2nd ed. Champaign, IL: Human Kinetics, 2003.

Fahey, Thomas D. *Weight Training Basics.* New York: McGraw-Hill, 2005.

Orvis, James. *Weight Training Workouts That Work.* Farmingham, MN: Ideal Publishing, 2000.

Sandler, David. *Weight Training Fundamentals: A Better Way to Learn the Basics.* Champaign, IL: Human Kinetics, 2003.

Schuler, Lou, and Ian King. *Men's Health: The Book of Muscle.* Emmaus, PA: Rodale Books, 2003.

Schoenfeld, Brad. *Sculpting Her Body Perfect.* 2nd ed. Champaign, IL: Human Kinetics, 2002.

Nutrition

Applegate, Liz. *Encyclopedia of Sports and Fitness Nutrition.* New York: Prima Lifestyles, 2002.

Clark, Nancy. *Nancy Clark's Sports Nutrition Guidebook.* 3rd ed. Champaign, IL: Human Kinetics, 2003.

Gastelu, Daniel, and Fred Hatfield. *Dynamic Nutrition for Maximum Performance: A Complete Nutritional Guide for Peak Sports Performance.* New York: Avery Publishing Group, 1997.

Hatfield, Fredrick C. *Nature's Sports Pharmacy.* New York: McGraw-Hill, 1999.

Netzer, Corinne T. *The Complete Book of Food Counts.* 6th ed. New York: Dell, 2003.

Periodicals

Fitness, fitnessmagazine.com

Flex, flexonline.com

Muscle and Fitness, muscle-fitness.com

Muscle and Fitness, Hers, muscleandfitnesshers.com

Men's Fitness, mensfitness.com

Men's Health, menshealth.com

Muscular Development, musculardevelopment.com

Natural Bodybuilding and Fitness, getbig.com

Natural Muscle, naturalmuscle.net

Internet Resources

American College of Sports Medicine (ACSM), acsm.org

A well-respected fitness organization that promotes the education and application of exercise science and sports medicine. The website offers a personal trainer locator and up-to-date fitness resources and articles.

American Council on Exercise (ACE), acefitness.org

A nonprofit organization committed to enriching quality of life through safe and effective physical activity. Its website provides fitness information and a personal trainer locator.

National Strength and Conditioning Association (NSCA), nsca-lift.org

The NSCA provides reliable, research-based strength and conditioning information to its members and the general public. There is an NSCA personal trainer locator on the website, as well as fitness articles and resources.

Food and Nutrition Information Center (FNIC), nal.usda.gov/fnic

This U.S. government website offers printable educational materials, government reports, research papers, and more. See also the U.S. Department of Agriculture Nutrient Database at nal.usda.gov/fnic/cgi-bin/nut_search.pl.

Tufts University Nutrition Navigator, http://navigator.tufts.edu

Tufts University, a name long respected among nutrition professionals, provides this site that lists and rates hundreds of nutrition websites that have been reviewed by its advisory board.

About the Author

A competitive swimmer, runner, and triathlete, Tim Houts has authored six fitness books with more than 200,000 copies in print for triathlon, running, strength training, and more.

Tim swam competitively beginning in grade school and went on to play water polo at Stanford University. Since college, he has run three marathons as well as numerous 10Ks and triathlons. Through all his training efforts, Tim has used strength training to supplement his time in the pool or on the road.